Bandana Wasteland

poems

Carly Bryson

NeoPoiesis Press, LLC

NeoPoiesis Press
P.O. Box 38037
Houston, TX 77238-8037

www.neopoiesispress.com

Copyright © 2012 by Carly Bryson

All rights reserved. No part of this book may be used or reproduced in any manner whatsoever without express written permission from the publisher except in the case of brief quotations embodied in critical articles and reviews.

Carly Bryson – Bandana Wasteland
ISBN 978-0-9832747-7-3 (paperback : alk. paper)
    1. Poetry. I. Bryson, Carly

Printed in the United States of America.

First Edition

For my son Dylan who teaches me every day the meaning of truly unconditional love

Contents

Texas is Burning 1
Atchafalaya 2
let me write as a river 3
down the wormhole 4
Windchimes of the Lost 6
Enough 7
December 8
Baytown 9
Maggot Farm 10
The Politics of Dreams 11
The Bastard Hive 12
A Killing Wind 13
Death Valley Twilight 14
How the World Ends 15
Chattel 16
The cool days were short lived 17
Until 18
Pretend 19
Leaving 20
father: your son is not dead 21
Limbo 22
I am Jane Doe 23
Waiting 24
Collapsed 25
500 Miles 26
Shatter 27
dirt 28
Gumbo 29
Portals 30
Karmic 31
More than a Mind 32
Net 33

Texas is Burning

Texas is burning--from the high plains
to the bluebonnet dressed hills
mesquite and ocatillo smolder and hiss
on desert roadsides
the fried empty sky fills with pillows
of blue-black smoke.

A million acres of fire, a legacy
of crumbled ashen homes,
charred shells of cars and machinery
fueled by a careless touch and dust bowl winds.

The cracked earth lies torched and blackened,
the dirt once starved for rain,
now too parched for salvation.

Atchafalaya

cypress knees, gnarled and broken
jut out just above the water's surface

random intervals of little silences
speak louder than dissonance

streams of days pass
little changes

at dawn the dragonflies
alight on the glass surface
wings transparent in early mist

the sun blinded by clouds
casts gauze shadows
on moss levees

near the banks
a thousand bones
lie beneath the gumbo dirt

babies--soldiers--slaves
sleep in shallow tombs
waiting for the earth to change

let me write as a river

let me write as a river Lord
let me carve history into canyons
snake and meander
move stealthily through this world
ribbon through gulches and gullies
let the rapids toss whitecaps on rivulets
just beneath the surface on days of laze and calm
as the bottom silt settles into bones
and the reeds rise high against the banks
let me flow from source to mouth
from sediment to delta
I'll strain against the levee
still and brackish in the sun

down the wormhole

then post industrialism became full bloom
widget factories sat dormant
long since farmed out to cheap labor
in hideous underbellies of exotic locales

the age of information was the new innovation
thriving mightily for a short while
turning paupers into barons
replacing goods with services

the family farm was assimilated by conglomerates
tractors and combines rusted in wheat fields
or sold as collectibles at auction
land no longer had to sustain its inhabitants
it only had to stock the grocer's shelves

labor was replaced by knowledge
knowledge absorbed marketable goods
and the process was thought convivial
consumers proliferated
instant gratification the new staple

they soaked up information and cheap Asian goods
marketers plugged into psyches
virtual reality was now reality
want replaced need for decades
until the dam broke under the weight of its own greed

war became a commodity to export like grain
money changers created need through fear
leaders and politicians became mediums

beyond the paradigm the next wave looms
maybe the distraction of fires floods and storms
super inflation, currency devaluation, police states
will shock quietly so it's barely even noticed

Windchimes of the Lost

Tonight I walk along the winding banks of a bayou
where a body was floating yesterday
tossed into it as refuse,
it rose to the top like cream on tea.

Men stand in shadows, pissing into bushes,
vomiting the last of the wine on empty stomachs.
One sits leaning against the trunk of a live oak,
his dreads wider than his emaciated frame.

Tooth loss has left hollow cheeks
and his arms are the size of his skeleton.
He shakes his cup and it jangles--
the wind chimes of the lost.

People walk around him a few extra feet
making sure not to get too close,
as if his living death might attach itself to them
or steal away their dreams--
he stares ahead, probably not noticing anyway.

Enough

Some days your body needs the sun.
You sit with your feet in the pool
moving your toes shark-like
watching the water ripple,
and you think it is too much, *this calm.*

You look beneath the surface
 for the jagged teeth,
your own bloated reflection,
lips mouthing silent O's.

You wonder if this is *enough.*

December

So the earth cools to a frigid end,
leaves crumble to powder,
spoken words trail into frozen vapor.

Old ones crackle like twigs on fire,
with eyes as bleak as winter.

In cemeteries,
where limbs of bare trees
gnarl arthritically against the sky,

they look for loved ones lost
or love misplaced,

they place paltry weeds on lonely graves,
to dream of youth and warmth,

instead of this sepulcher--
this tomb--this cold December

Baytown

May's air is heavy,
with the salt mist of the gulf.

A thousand man hours of chemical waste
dances in the sky beneath the cloud borders.

At night driving down the old Baytown highway,
you see the lights of the refineries.

A small city of storage tanks, processors
and cooling towers illuminate the night sky.

Tall smokestacks emit odorous vapor
of sulphur and petroleum that makes
you want to scratch your skin until it bleeds.

Just beyond that five mile stretch
an inlet to the ocean lies beneath the bridge.

You hold your breath and just drive.

Maggot Farm

There is blood in this machine
this place that once
stood proud and unyielding,
once unlimited potential
lies stagnant and putrid.

We are the cowards who
tilled the maggot farm
carefully cultivating each ovum
generation after generation
creating a dream that
never had a chance to survive.

We are the liars
who perpetrated the deception
that hard work was honest
and honesty meant progress
while progress was sold to
the highest bidder because
it was just easier to become refuse.

We are the larva peddlers
who thought that giving away power
meant giving away blame
so we sit oblivious or wallowing
waiting for sickness or death
to induce us to stop devouring our own.

The Politics of Dreams

I am neither here nor there
my heart split as my mind

I never bought the world as it is
I find fascination with what it was

before the fixes that fixed us
when a man's honor was his shield

when we could look around
and say there's happiness here

before greed became the politics of dreams
and a good night's sleep was taken for granted

The Bastard Hive

To stand alone in shorn fields wilting
sun tears and sorrow,
measuring a soul's worth in pennies.

Felled by hours light shadows tilting
laid on day's morrow,
filled vast this vessel of tyranny.

Sweat drenched beside angels black dresses
alone but for a glance,
hands cracked with lines of penance and fate
eyes veiled by straying sodden tresses
pleading out lost chance
silence embeds in forever slate.

Truth will die in whimpering twilight
doubted seeds survive,
we will stand in this blood seeped madness
uncrying we'll watch the death knell light.

Let the bastard hive shovel the graves
with dirt and sadness.

A Killing Wind

The tanks rolled again
toward someone's
version of freedom.

When winter came, the ground
covered in snow and glass,
hungered for the color of poppies
replaced by thorn in stone.

The sky fell to Earth
danced in on blue-white smoke,
the gusts of a killing wind.

Death Valley Twilight

The sky's eerie glow
washed over the desert
darkening the whitest sand,
we drove another twenty miles
with three hundred more to go,
pulled over when we lost the light
on the crackled serpentine road.

Too arid to sweat,
the heat pounded our heads
to the point we couldn't sleep,
we put damp blankets on the ground
and prayed for sweet relief.

We watched the Milky Way
splayed across the constellations,
the sky's usual black gave way
to a charcoaled blue,
contaminated by far off city lights.

The tümpisa, land of the Timbisha,
laid still unbathed in darkest night.

How the World Ends

The wind shrieks full circle
tree branches twist in the window.

I burrow deep into my asylum
eyes pried open beneath the sheets.

I won't be the biographer of the apocalypse
and it won't come like you think.

No sudden fissures to swallow us up
when we back the car out of the garage.

It will be slow tears in the fabric of the world
we'll hear them in the background every day.

They'll hum unnoticed doing their damage
while we go to work, pay the bills.

We'll raise kids, cook dinner, make love
lose loved ones, grow older.

When we can no longer speak out or pray
or curse the silent gods.

Dystopia--gradual and insidious
will creep along spineless roads and fill forgotten skies.

Reserve the bagpipes,
"Whispering Hope" will be the theme to world's end.

Chattel

In a moment of exemption
lay down the broken bows
rest from this dystopia
this deprivation
chattel of the street

flick the flies from bony backs
swaddled in the heat
scrap with sparrows for crumbs
leave the sorrow for later
if later ever comes

The cool days were short lived

The cool days were short lived
replaced by early morning swelter
I see it bounce off the pavement
delusional oasis waves
dance across my hood.

Lord I'm losing my mind,
my poor baked bundt cake brain
whatever it processes these days,
immediately suspect.

The years are expert at dismantling,
flesh, cartilage, bone, matter
layer after layer building
toward an impressive ruin.

That strong girl is gone,
the backbone bank ran dry
no bailouts, no dividends
no tiptoeing gingerly across the timeline,
no reverse.

I tell myself *remember these days*
of iced teas and sunstrokes
to wrap around my arms
when the chill comes.

Until

May to October blends
together in these parts
what the sun doesn't blister
the humidity wilts

sparrows whistle in dawn
the cicadas deafen dusk
with plaintive rings

the noise of a busy planet
whirs down the asphalt
tacky from the heat
rutted from the weight of progress

oppression is not always
a social condition
sometimes it sits in the air
fused by a hundred days of sameness
but always waiting

until the gentle cleanse
of an afternoon rain
wipes the chalklines from sheets
cakes the rust on cherry pickers
lining the pummeled streets

until tar soaked caliche crumbles
beneath shoeless feet,
and air is lifted for a moment
in defiance of tradition

Pretend

I pretend I am seven again
I can do a standing backbend,
bringing my legs smoothly over
placing them on the ground.

Twist me like a double helix
ravage me with pain that never forgets
you lie buried within this sinewy
passage of tendon and cartilage
burning from the inside.
I want to chew you like a jerky treat
so you can feel like me when I spit you out.

Mom says I laugh like a hyena
and I run as fast as I can
back straight and carefree.

I play energetically on the grass
turning round and round in circles
reaching for the sky
touching my tongue to a cloud.

Leaving

A whistle into the wind echoes
from one county to the next,
where slate highways lull in linear silence
along a million years of oil and sand,
the night noiseless but for a cicada's lyrical pulse.

The moon, a chrome half sphere in the dark distance,
casts a cool wash over the blacktop.
Lightning bugs make luminarias
of roadside weeds and shrubs.

Something reels toward you,
you don't know it exists.
It moves, you flinch and it disappears.

You left with a dream and a mother's prayer,
a hundred miles away the stench remains.
This night, the leaving, a thing of beauty,
holds the remainder of what still shines.

You drive into the mystery of things
toward the quiet shadows,
where moire curtains of stars pellet the horizon.

father: your son is not dead

father, your son is not dead, he is dying
each night the eyes appear closed from the loft roof

sleeping princes never cry

worms could crawl across those thin arms
he wouldn't flinch

little boy, little man

you'd never hear him if he did,
you were always deaf if not blind

I hear the hush and rasp, not wanting to smother
I die each day in pieces yet you seem to survive

Limbo

I could fall face first into the earth,
crack open the dirt
watch ants serpentine over my skin,

Not alive but not quite dead,
but somewhere in between,

in limbo lies a map for the flies,
this life will be the death of me.

I am Jane Doe

The ground is so dry
fireflies set off small grass fires
in sidewalk cracks

I am in the episode of Twilight Zone
where the earth is off its axis
hurling perilously close to the sun

I am the old woman sitting
at her apartment window
wiping sweat from her face
with a warm damp cloth
praying for salvation
from a God no longer listening

Waiting for all traces
of flesh and memory
to melt away

I am Jane Doe
a human carcass
lying tempered on the floor
too wet for the chalk outline

Waiting

It wasn't his body but a shell containing
ten years of indiscretions mistaken for love.

He laid in the hospital bed every other month
like a rotting seed pod, hollow and rattling,
a specimen poked and stuck
with the mercy of clinical trials,

His eyes, slits or slots, open long enough
to see another yellow swab stuffed into the bin;
awake long enough to hear the hushed mumbling
of doctor to nurse each time wondering if they
were discussing his cell count or the weather.

Was it cloudy or just the darkness of the sun
muted through tinted glass?

His frame so thin when he coughed his chest
caved more than heaved, and weren't we lucky
to find a good vein today?

The slots closed once again, the pod folded,
the stemmed head crushed, dropped to the dirt.

Collapsed

What was it you said to me
in a moment of contrition, or stupor
beneath the glow of a lone streetlamp?

The moon sketches
a graffiti of light atop the macadam,
casting our young spare frames
into chalk outlines.

Was it something about past or future?
Something that seemed out of place
in a romance still green and uncured,
the slight soon forgotten when that first belly rush
was mistaken for something resembling love.

A passing car splashed mud,
the moment collapsed.

500 Miles

Death is a highway in the Trans-Pecos
where painted white road perforations
blur into single lines.

At night, prehistoric things fly into the windshield
until the wipers have smeared it so badly
you have to pull over somewhere
in the five hundred miles
between nothing and nowhere.

There are no carwashes in Hell,
just a two pump gas station
stuck so far back in time
you can't fill your own tank
and forget about a credit card slot.

You want to order a sandwich inside
but the cat perched atop the counter
suddenly turns your stomach
at the thought of barbeque and fur balls.

Dawn begins creeping over the low mesas
and you stand outside your car
as the wind blows dirt into your mouth.

The kind of grit only a cold cerveza will wash away
but you can't buy it until noon
so you grab a lukewarm soda from the back seat
where it's nestled between a tote bag
and a half eaten bag of Doritos.

Just a half day left of Chihuahuan desert...

Shatter

Shatter these days
into pieces of kaleidoscope glass,

dash-dot-dot-dash
across wind burned fields
leaving ashen footprints in dry earth
for our children's children
to dissect as if it mattered,

as if the circle never closes
and these leavings
will not seem to the future
like another pile of historical sludge,

the colors smeared gray with time
will fade from the sky
and from our eyes,

beyond two generations
no one will care
about decomposing snapshots
lying in the bottom of cedar chests,
or the lives they represent.

dirt

i want to breathe in
your acrid air
burn my lungs in your
bandana wasteland

unstick my flesh
from melted vinyl
at every stop between
here and there

swig down a Crush
throw a bill to a beggar
and wash away his dust

find the long dirt road
holds the stones behind my eyes
and the bones that fill my dreams

drive a thousand hours
where crows wait in gravel
i see it in my sleep

Gumbo

A city built on gumbo

defying gravity
year after year
saved only by the
forethought of some
prolific engineer.

I wonder if Atlantis
started this way?

Soil never meant
to sustain steel and pavement
bubbles up with each rain
and the next.

Two hundred years
of gooey silt
hides beneath
manmade dreams
that never worked.

If it weren't for reservoirs

the bayous straining their muddy guts
would be lakes now
and fish would be commuters.

Portals

Transporters of choice,
open roads, open windows, open doors.

Horizons are dream portals
full of possibility or quiet dread.

Does it even matter how our molecules
get from here to there?

Trees fly by, flecks in the landscape
Of course we fly as they stand still.

The moving fields,
we never see them nor care.

Stare ahead, blinders secured
traveling like shadows into the sun.

Karmic

The damage we do will outlive us all
yet we are still in our savagery--
complicit in our denial.

I see faces in the wreckage,
each pixel made of flesh and history.

If only we took the same care
as with a simple caress
but like a delicate arm, she bruises well.

The truth will be a scythe-the dirt a path
and the story, how progress prevailed
wrapped in flags and apple pies,
how we embraced the disease without diagnosis,
eating the sugar cube placebos.

The stone shifters knew their stuff,
we revered them but even their pillars
won't survive the shifting plates
when the seeds are gone, the roots will perish
our resilience will lie in karmic purgatory
reduced once again to simple matter.

More than a Mind

Forty years of bad luck
subterfuge as you watched the game
had babies, got shitfaced, shot zombies

great minds weren't made like this
knowledge costs more than money
lack of costs more than a mind.

now gather that collective wasteland
turn wishes to diamonds and toss to the sky
minutes become days until you smell of piss

sing your Lazarus songs.
leave your refuse to the match
light it up and burn it down

time and the universe don't care
we go on alone

Net

He brandished his smile like a silk harpoon
not spear-like, but capable of impalement
capture certain if I were capturable
or gullible or guard-down stupid

I would have been winched up
like a billowy jib
hoisted by the fair winds
trapped in a silk-web net
flailing, fists clenched as he circled about

but the swells caught him
distracted enough I looked away
from those depths into the cove
beyond thc whitecaps
where the calm blue bore no siren
to draw the net ashore

Acknowledgements

The following poems have been previously published:

500 Miles, *Calliope Nerve*
Baytown, *Calliope Nerve*
Gumbo, *Calliope Nerve*
Karmic, *Virgogray Press*
The Bastard Hive, *ETC: A Journal of General Semantics*
Waiting, *Virgogray Press*
Windchimes of the Lost, *Red Fez*

About the Author

Carly Bryson is a native Texan raised in the oilfields of west Texas somewhere between the Edwards Plateau and the Guadalajara desert. Currently residing in Houston, she writes poetry and prose dealing with politics, current events, nature, and family dynamics.

She has been published in Carcinogenic Poetry, Calliope Nerve, The Shine Journal, ETC: A Review of General Semantics, as well as two anthologies, and NothingNoOneNowhere.

Banduna Wasteland is her first collection of poetry and contains poems which address an increasingly dystopic and Orwellian society forming amidst an age of war, disinformation, media bias, environmental decline and propaganda.

NeoPoiesis: *a new way of making*

1) in ancient Greece, poiesis referred to the process of making: creation - production - organization - formation - causation

2) a process that can be physical and spiritual, biological and intellectual, artistic and technological, material and teleological, efficient and formal

3) a means of modifying the environment and a method of organizing the self, the making of art and music and poetry, the fashioning of memory and history and philosophy, the construction of perception and expression and reality

4) an independent publisher with a steadfast goal to print and promote outstanding poets, writers and artists that reflect the creative drive and spirit of the new electronic landscape

NeoPoiesisPress.com

www.ingramcontent.com/pod-product-compliance
Lightning Source LLC
Chambersburg PA
CBHW051719040426
42446CB00008B/967